TRD · MRK

ALPHABETS · FLOURISHES · ORNAMENTS

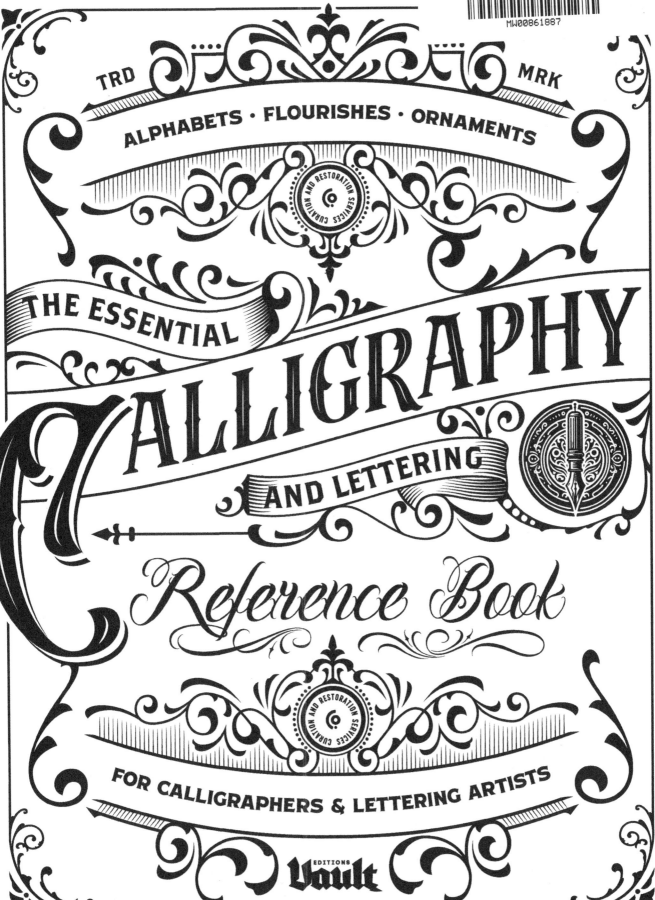

THE ESSENTIAL

# CALLIGRAPHY

AND LETTERING

*Reference Book*

FOR CALLIGRAPHERS & LETTERING ARTISTS

EDITIONS Vault

## 01
**VOLUME**

# INTRODUCTION

**BIBLIOGRAPHICAL NOTE**

This publication is a new work by Vault Editions Ltd.

**AUTHOR**

This publication was curated and authored by Kale James.

# PREFACE

By Kale James

Welcome to *The Essential Calligraphy and Hand Lettering Reference Book*, a treasure trove for enthusiasts of the written word's beauty and form. This book is a culmination of admiration and respect for the art of calligraphy and hand lettering, an art that intertwines history, design, and personal expression in unique ways that continue to captivate and inspire.

This book is a curated collection of historical references, meticulously gathered from the 18th and 19th centuries—a period rich in artistic innovation and excellence. These references were produced by some of the world's most esteemed calligraphers, whose work has set the standards of beauty and skill for generations to follow. As you turn the pages, you will embark on a journey through time, exploring blackletter alphabets, ornamental and cursive scripts, and intricate flourish art depicting animals such as eagles, dragons, swans, deer, fish, horses, and songbirds. Each piece is a testament to the mastery and creative vision of its creator.

This publication is designed not just to showcase these historical masterpieces but also to serve as a practical guide for today's calligraphers, hand lettering artists, typographers, and designers. Whether you are a beginner eager to learn the basics or an experienced artist seeking to refine your technique and draw inspiration from the masters, you will find valuable resources within these pages. The inclusion of flourishing exercises and a collection of ornamental page elements like cartouches, frames, and borders offers you the tools to elevate your own work, blending tradition with your personal style.

Each book includes a download code for high-resolution images of all featured works, allowing detailed study and inspiration.

*The Essential Calligraphy and Hand Lettering Reference Book* is more than a compilation; it is an invitation to explore, learn, and continue the legacy of calligraphy and hand lettering. It celebrates the past while looking forward to the new meanings and expressions that you, as an artist, will contribute to this timeless typographic art form.

We hope this book becomes a cherished tool in your artistic journey as you draw inspiration from the world's masters to forge your path in the enchanting world of calligraphy and hand lettering. Welcome to your journey of discovery, creativity, and mastery.

| PUBLISHER | ISBN | |
|---|---|---|
| Vault Editions Ltd<br>vaulteditions.com | 978-1-922966-35-3 | vau |

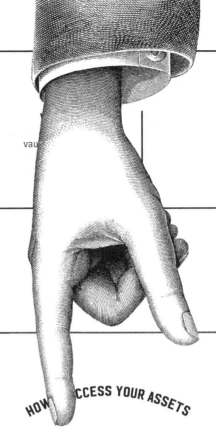

# TABLE OF CONTENTS

# ACKNOWLEDGMENTS

In the creation of *The Essential Calligraphy and Hand Lettering Reference Book*, we stand on the shoulders of giants—artists whose skill, vision, and dedication to the craft of calligraphy and penmanship have transcended time. It is with deep gratitude and respect that we acknowledge and celebrate the master calligraphers and penmen whose work is featured within these pages.

Their contributions to the art of calligraphy and hand lettering have enriched our cultural heritage and provided an endless source of inspiration and learning for current and future generations. Their work's beauty, complexity, and elegance remind us of the power of the written word and the timeless appeal of artistic excellence.

We extend our sincerest thanks to the descendants and caretakers of these artists' legacies, who have graciously allowed us to share these historical treasures with a wider audience. Their willingness

Access to these masterpieces ensures that the artistry and techniques of the past continue to inform and inspire the work of contemporary calligraphers and lettering enthusiasts.

This book is a tribute to the enduring legacy of these remarkable artists. Through their work, we are reminded of the boundless potential of human creativity and the unifying power of art across generations. Our heartfelt appreciation goes out to each of these artists, without whom this book would not have been possible. May their work continue to inspire, educate, and delight all who have the privilege of beholding it.

## HOW TO ACCESS YOUR ASSETS

# DOWNLOAD YOUR FILES

### DIGITISED FILES AVAILABLE

**INSTRUCTIONS TO DOWNLOAD THE FILES ARE LOCATED ON THE FINAL PAGE OF THIS PUBLICATION. GO GET'EM!**

WITH HIGH RESOLUTION DOWNLOAD!

# CONTACT

Do you need assistance accessing your files? Or do you have a questions about our products and services? If so, our team will be more than happy to help you. Please contact Vault Editions via: info@vaulteditions.com

# 300 DPI
## IND STANDARD

# DESIGNED IN LONDON

· DESIGNER ·
E. L. BROWN

CALLIGRAPHY
*And* HAND LETTERING

· TYPEFACE ·
OLD ENGLISH

UPPER & LOWER CASE ← → WEIGHT: REGULAR ← → PUBLISHED: C. 1900

01

ABCDEFGHIJKL
MNOPQRSTU
VWXYZ&Et
abcdefghijklmnop
qrstuvwxyz

Old English

1

A HIGH RESOLUTION FILE OF THIS SPECIMEN SHEET CAN BE DOWNLOADED FROM THE VAULT EDITIONS' WEBSITE.

*Vault Editions Ltd*

PRACTICE
T R D  MAKES  M R K
PERFECT

INDUSTRY STD

VAULTEDITIONS.COM

·DESIGNER·

E. L. BROWN

CALLIGRAPHY
And HAND LETTERING

·TYPEFACE·

BLACKLETTER: UNTITLED

UPPER & LOWER CASE ←→ WEIGHT: REGULAR ←→ PUBLISHED: C. 1900

02

2

A HIGH RESOLUTION FILE OF THIS
SPECIMEN SHEET CAN BE DOWNLOADED
FROM THE VAULT EDITIONS' WEBSITE.

Vault Editions Ltd

TRD PRACTICE MAKES PERFECT MRK

INDUSTRY STD

VAULTEDITIONS.COM

·DESIGNER·

D. W. EDWARD

# CALLIGRAPHY
*And* HAND LETTERING

·TYPEFACE·

RAPID BROAD PEN
GERMAN TEXT

UPPER | LOWER | NUMERALS ← → | WEIGHT: REGULAR | ← → | PUBLISHED: 1859

03

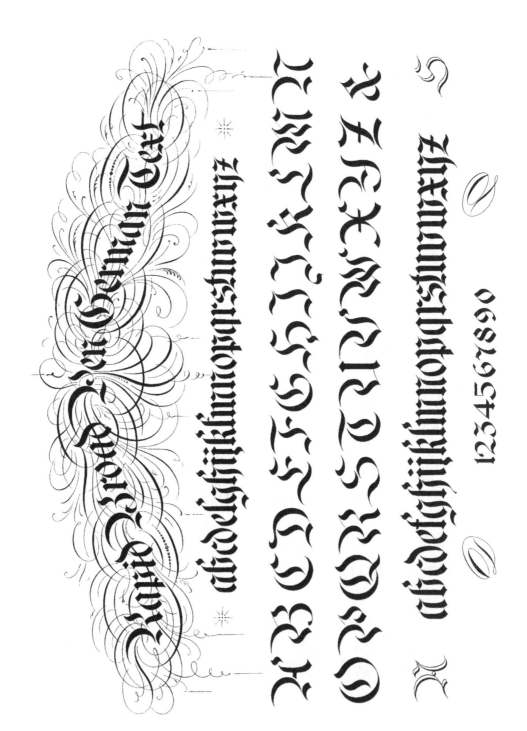

3

A HIGH RESOLUTION FILE OF THIS
SPECIMEN SHEET CAN BE DOWNLOADED
FROM THE VAULT EDITIONS' WEBSITE.

*Vault Editions Ltd*

PRACTICE
MAKES
PERFECT

INDUSTRY STD

VAULTEDITIONS.COM

·DESIGNER·

D. W. EDWARD

# CALLIGRAPHY
## And HAND LETTERING

·TYPEFACE·

**RAPID EXTENDED
OLD ENGLISH**

UPPER | LOWER | NUMERALS ⟷ WEIGHT: REGULAR ⟷ PUBLISHED: 1859

04

4

A HIGH RESOLUTION FILE OF THIS
SPECIMEN SHEET CAN BE DOWNLOADED
FROM THE VAULT EDITIONS' WEBSITE.

*Vault Editions Ltd*

PRACTICE
MAKES
PERFECT

INDUSTRY STD

VAULTEDITIONS.COM

·DESIGNER·
E. L BROWN

# CALLIGRAPHY
*And* HAND LETTERING

·TYPEFACE·
BLACKLETTER: UNTITLED

UPPER & LOWER CASE ←→ WEIGHT: REGULAR ←→ PUBLISHED: C. 1900

05

5

A HIGH RESOLUTION FILE OF THIS
SPECIMEN SHEET CAN BE DOWNLOADED
FROM THE VAULT EDITIONS' WEBSITE.

*Vault Editions Ltd*

PRACTICE
MAKES
PERFECT

INDUSTRY STD

VAULTEDITIONS.COM

·DESIGNER·
E. L BROWN

CALLIGRAPHY
And HAND LETTERING

·TYPEFACE·
RETOUCHED OLD ENGLISH

UPPER | LOWER | NUMERALS   WEIGHT: REGULAR   PUBLISHED: C. 1900

06

## Retouched Old English

abcdefghijklmnopqrstuvwxyz

ABCDEFGHIJKLMNO

PQRRSTUVWXYZ&A

aadgqi 1234567890ß hvwyyſ

— LUPFER —

abcdefghijklmnopqr

stuvwxyz12345678

90ABCDEFGHI

JKLMNOPQRS

TUVWXYZ&C?

6

A HIGH RESOLUTION FILE OF THIS
SPECIMEN SHEET CAN BE DOWNLOADED
FROM THE VAULT EDITIONS' WEBSITE.

Vault Editions Ltd

PRACTICE
MAKES
PERFECT

INDUSTRY STD

VAULTEDITIONS.COM

·DESIGNER·

E. L BROWN

CALLIGRAPHY
And HAND LETTERING

·TYPEFACE·

OLD ENGLISH

07

7

A HIGH RESOLUTION FILE OF THIS
SPECIMEN SHEET CAN BE DOWNLOADED
FROM THE VAULT EDITIONS' WEBSITE.

Vault Editions Ltd

CURATION AND RESTORATION SERVICES ©

PRACTICE
T R D MAKES M R K
PERFECT

INDUSTRY STD

VAULTEDITIONS.COM

·DESIGNER·

E. L BROWN

CALLIGRAPHY
And HAND LETTERING

·TYPEFACE·

BLACHLETTER: UNTITLED

UPPER | LOWER | NUMERALS ← → WEIGHT: REGULAR ← → PUBLISHED: C. 1900

08

8

A HIGH RESOLUTION FILE OF THIS
SPECIMEN SHEET CAN BE DOWNLOADED
FROM THE VAULT EDITIONS' WEBSITE.

Vault Editions Ltd

PRACTICE
MAKES
PERFECT

INDUSTRY STD

VAULTEDITIONS.COM

·DESIGNER·

G. A. GASHELL

CALLIGRAPHY
And HAND LETTERING

·TYPEFACE·

GERMAN TEXT

09

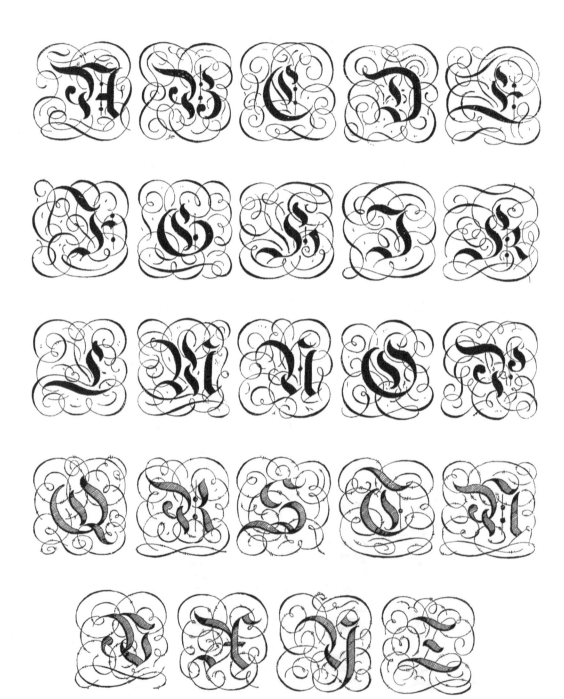

PRACTICE
MAKES
PERFECT

T R D    M R K

INDUSTRY STD

VAULTEDITIONS.COM

·DESIGNER.
C. P. ZANER

CALLIGRAPHY
And HAND LETTERING

·TYPEFACE.
RAPID OLD ENGLISH
EXTENDED CHARACTERS

UPPER & LOWER CASE ←→ WEIGHT: REGULAR ←→ PUBLISHED: 1897

10

Vault Editions Ltd

CURATION AND RESTORATION SERVICES

PRACTICE MAKES PERFECT
T·R·D    M·R·K

INDUSTRY STD

VAULTEDITIONS.COM

·DESIGNER·

E. L BROWN

# CALLIGRAPHY
*And* HAND LETTERING

·TYPEFACE·

QUILL PEN,
GERMAN TEXT

UPPER CASE ← → WEIGHT: REGULAR ← → PUBLISHED: C. 1900

11

*Vault Editions Ltd*

CURATION AND RESTORATION SERVICES

PRACTICE
T R D   MAKES   M R K
PERFECT

INDUSTRY STD

VAULTEDITIONS.COM

·DESIGNER·
E. L. BROWN

CALLIGRAPHY
And HAND LETTERING

·TYPEFACE·
OLD ENGLISH

UPPER | LOWER | NUMERALS　　WEIGHT: REGULAR　　PUBLISHED: C. 1900

12

Old English

12345

A HIGH RESOLUTION FILE OF THIS SPECIMEN SHEET CAN BE DOWNLOADED FROM THE VAULT EDITIONS' WEBSITE.

Vault Editions Ltd

PRACTICE MAKES PERFECT

INDUSTRY STD

VAULTEDITIONS.COM

·DESIGNER·
E. L BROWN

# CALLIGRAPHY
*And* HAND LETTERING

·TYPEFACE·
ORNAMENTAL GERMAN
TEXT

UPPER CASE ⟷ WEIGHT: REGULAR ⟷ PUBLISHED: C. 1900

13

*Vault Editions Ltd*

PRACTICE
T R D    MAKES    M R K
PERFECT

INDUSTRY STD

VAULTEDITIONS.COM

**CALLIGRAPHY**
*And* HAND LETTERING

**UPPER & LOWER CASE** ⟷ **WEIGHT: REGULAR** ⟷ **PUBLISHED: C. 1900**

14

*Vault Editions Ltd*

PRACTICE
T R D MAKES M R K
PERFECT

INDUSTRY STD

VAULTEDITIONS.COM

·DESIGNER·
E. L BROWN

CALLIGRAPHY
And HAND LETTERING

·TYPEFACE·
CHURCH STYLE

UPPER & LOWER CASE ⟷ WEIGHT: REGULAR ⟷ PUBLISHED: C. 1900

15

Vault Editions Ltd

PRACTICE
MAKES
PERFECT
TRD MRK

INDUSTRY STD

VAULTEDITIONS.COM

CALLIGRAPHY
And HAND LETTERING

UPPER & LOWER CASE ⟷ WEIGHT: REGULAR ⟷ PUBLISHED: C. 1900

16

Vault Editions Ltd

PRACTICE
T R D MAKES M R K
PERFECT

INDUSTRY STD

VAULTEDITIONS.COM

·PUBLISHER·
KNOWLES & MAXIM

CALLIGRAPHY
And HAND LETTERING

·TYPEFACE·
GERMAN TEXT

UPPER & LOWER CASE &larr; &rarr; WEIGHT: REGULAR &larr; &rarr; PUBLISHED: 1881

17

Vault Editions Ltd

PRACTICE
MAKES
PERFECT

INDUSTRY STD

VAULTEDITIONS.COM

.PUBLISHER.
HNOWLES & MAXIM

CALLIGRAPHY
And HAND LETTERING

.TYPEFACE.
OLD ENGLISH

18

ABCDEFGHIJKLM
NOPQRSTUVWXYZ
abcdefghijklmnopqrstuvwxyz

Vault Editions Ltd

PRACTICE
MAKES
PERFECT

INDUSTRY STD

VAULTEDITIONS.COM

·PUBLISHER·
LAIRD & LEE

CALLIGRAPHY
*And* HAND LETTERING

·TYPEFACE·
OLD ENGLISH CAPTIALS

UPPER & LOWER CASE ⟷ WEIGHT: REGULAR ⟷ PUBLISHED: 1859

19

A B C D E F G

H I J K L M N

O P Q R S T U

V W X Y Z abc

defghijklmnop

qrstuvwxyz

19

A HIGH RESOLUTION FILE OF THIS
SPECIMEN SHEET CAN BE DOWNLOADED
FROM THE VAULT EDITIONS' WEBSITE.

Vault Editions Ltd

PRACTICE
MAKES
PERFECT
TRD · MRK

INDUSTRY STD

VAULTEDITIONS.COM

·PUBLISHER·
LAIRD & LEE

CALLIGRAPHY
And HAND LETTERING

·TYPEFACE·
MODIFIED OLD ENGLISH
TEXT

UPPER & LOWER CASE     WEIGHT: REGULAR     PUBLISHED: 1881

20

# ABCDEFGHI
# JKLMNOPQR
# STUVWXYZ.I
# abcdefghijkmn
# opqrstuvwxyz.
# 1234567890

Vault Editions Ltd

PRACTICE
TRD MAKES MRK
PERFECT

INDUSTRY STD

VAULTEDITIONS.COM

·PUBLISHER·
LAIRD & LEE

CALLIGRAPHY
*And* HAND LETTERING

·TYPEFACE·
GERMAN CAPITALS

UPPER & LOWER CASE ← → WEIGHT: REGULAR ← → PUBLISHED: 1859

21

A B C D E F
G H I J K L
M N O P Q
R S T U V
W X Y Z

a b c d e f g h i j k l m n
o p q r s t u v w x y z .

*Vault Editions Ltd*

PRACTICE
T R D   MAKES   M R K
PERFECT

INDUSTRY STD

VAULTEDITIONS.COM

.DESIGNER.
V. B. GRINNELL

CALLIGRAPHY
And HAND LETTERING

.TYPEFACE.
MODERN TEXT

22

Vault Editions Ltd

CURATION AND RESTORATION SERVICES

PRACTICE MAKES PERFECT
T R D     M R K

INDUSTRY STD

VAULTEDITIONS.COM

· DESIGNER ·
V. B. GRINNELL

# CALLIGRAPHY
## And HAND LETTERING

· TYPEFACE ·
SYLVAN TEXT

UPPER CASE ← → WEIGHT: REGULAR ← → PUBLISHED: 1859

23

Vault Editions Ltd

CURATION AND RESTORATION SERVICES

PRACTICE
MAKES
PERFECT
T R D
M R K

INDUSTRY STD

VAULTEDITIONS.COM

CALLIGRAPHY
And HAND LETTERING

24

a b c d e f g h i

j k l m n o p q r

s f t u v w r y z

1 2 3 4 5 6 7

8 9 0 · , &

Vault Editions Ltd

CURATION AND RESTORATION SERVICES

PRACTICE
T R D MAKES M R K
PERFECT

INDUSTRY STD

VAULTEDITIONS.COM

·DESIGNER·
V. B. GRINNELL

CALLIGRAPHY
And HAND LETTERING

·TYPEFACE·
STEELPLATE TEXT

UPPER & LOWER CASE ← → WEIGHT: REGULAR ← → PUBLISHED: 1859

25

A B C D E F G H
I K L M N O P Q
R S T U V W X Y
B . , & 1 2 3 4 5 6
7 8 9 0 a b c d e f
g h i j k l m n o p q
r s t u v w x y z

·DESIGNER·
V. B. GRINNELL

# CALLIGRAPHY
*And* HAND LETTERING

·TYPEFACE·
SHADED TEXT

UPPER & LOWER CASE   ← →   WEIGHT: REGULAR   ← →   PUBLISHED: C. 1890

26

*Vault Editions Ltd*

CURATION AND RESTORATION SERVICES

PRACTICE MAKES PERFECT
TRD
MRK

INDUSTRY STD

VAULTEDITIONS.COM

·DESIGNER·
C. A. FAUST

CALLIGRAPHY
And HAND LETTERING

·TYPEFACE·
GERMAN ALPHABETS

UPPER & LOWER CASE    WEIGHT: REGULAR    PUBLISHED: 1860

27

27

A HIGH RESOLUTION FILE OF THIS
SPECIMEN SHEET CAN BE DOWNLOADED
FROM THE VAULT EDITIONS' WEBSITE.

Vault Editions Ltd

PRACTICE
MAKES
PERFECT

INDUSTRY STD

VAULTEDITIONS.COM

CALLIGRAPHY
And HAND LETTERING

UPPER & LOWER CASE ←→ WEIGHT: REGULAR ←→ PUBLISHED: 1860

28

Vault Editions Ltd

CURATION AND RESTORATION SERVICES

PRACTICE
T R D MAKES M R K
PERFECT

INDUSTRY STD

VAULTEDITIONS.COM

.DESIGNER.
C. A. FAUST

CALLIGRAPHY
And HAND LETTERING

.TYPEFACE.
ENGRAVER'S FANCY
GERMAN TEXT

UPPER & LOWER CASE ←——→ WEIGHT: REGULAR ←——→ PUBLISHED: 1860

29

Vault Editions Ltd

PRACTICE
MAKES
PERFECT

INDUSTRY STD

VAULTEDITIONS.COM

**·DESIGNER·**
**ALBRECHT DURER**

**CALLIGRAPHY**
*And* **HAND LETTERING**

**·TYPEFACE·**
**ALBRECHT DURER'S LETTERS**

**UPPER & LOWER CASE**  **WEIGHT: REGULAR**  **PUBLISHED: 1860**

30

31

*Vault Editions Ltd*

PRACTICE MAKES PERFECT

INDUSTRY STD

VAULTEDITIONS.COM

.DESIGNER.
E. L. BROWN

CALLIGRAPHY
And HAND LETTERING

.TYPEFACE.
UNTITLED SCRIPT

UPPER | LOWER | NUMERALS    WEIGHT: REGULAR    PUBLISHED: C. 1900

32

a b c d e f f g g h i j k
l m n o p q r s t u v w x
y y z . 1 2 3 4 5 6 7 8 9

A A B B C D D
E E F F G G H H I
J K K L L M M M
N N O O P P Q Q
R R S S T T U U
V V V W W W W
X X Y Y Z Z Y

Vault Editions Ltd

PRACTICE
TRD MAKES MRK
PERFECT

INDUSTRY STD

VAULTEDITIONS.COM

·DESIGNER·
E. L. BROWN

CALLIGRAPHY
And HAND LETTERING

·TYPEFACE·
MONOGRAM LETTERS

UPPER CASE ← → WEIGHT: REGULAR ← → PUBLISHED: C. 1900

33

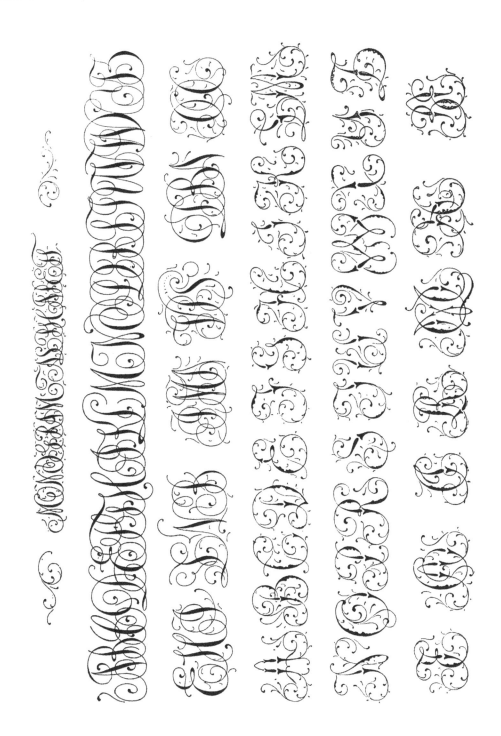

Vault Editions Ltd

CURATION AND RESTORATION SERVICES

PRACTICE
T R D   MAKES   M R K
PERFECT

INDUSTRY STD

VAULTEDITIONS.COM

·DESIGNER·

E. L. BROWN

# CALLIGRAPHY
*And* HAND LETTERING

·TYPEFACE·

UNTITLED SCRIPT

UPPER | LOWER | NUMERALS ⟵ ⟶ WEIGHT: REGULAR ⟵ ⟶ PUBLISHED: C. 1900

34

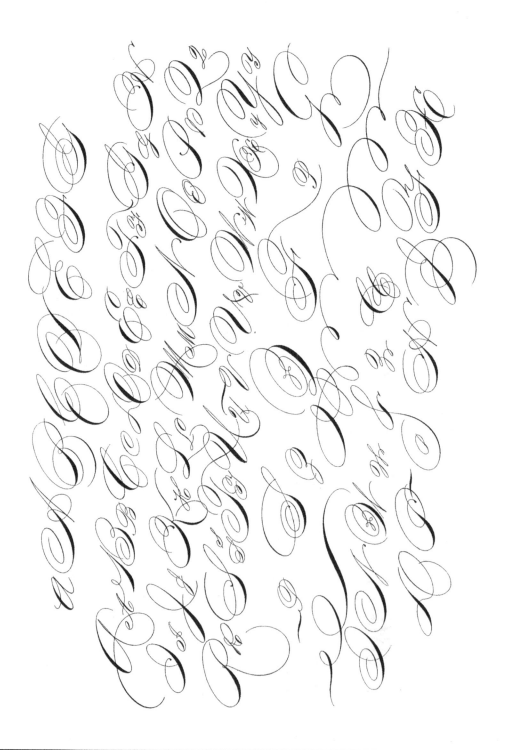

*Vault Editions Ltd*

PRACTICE
MAKES
PERFECT

INDUSTRY STD

VAULTEDITIONS.COM

.DESIGNER.

E. L. BROWN

CALLIGRAPHY
And HAND LETTERING

.TYPEFACE.

ENGRAVER'S SCRIPT

UPPER CASE ← → WEIGHT: REGULAR ← → PUBLISHED: C. 1900

35

Vault Editions Ltd

PRACTICE
MAKES
PERFECT

INDUSTRY STD

VAULTEDITIONS.COM

.DESIGNER.
E. L. BROWN

# CALLIGRAPHY
*And* HAND LETTERING

.TYPEFACE.
ITALIAN CAPITALS

UPPER CASE ←→ WEIGHT: REGULAR ←→ PUBLISHED: C. 1900

36

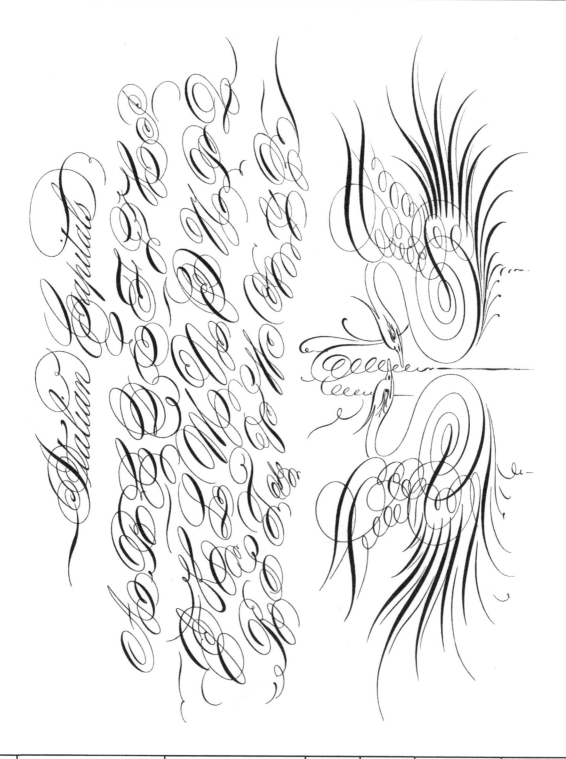

*Vault Editions Ltd*

PRACTICE
MAKES
PERFECT

INDUSTRY STD

VAULTEDITIONS.COM

.DESIGNER.

E. L. BROWN

# CALLIGRAPHY
*And* HAND LETTERING

.TYPEFACE.

UNTITLED SCRIPT

UPPER CASE ←→ WEIGHT: REGULAR ←→ PUBLISHED: C. 1900

37

*Vault Editions Ltd*

PRACTICE MAKES PERFECT

INDUSTRY STD

VAULTEDITIONS.COM

·DESIGNER·

E. L. BROWN

# CALLIGRAPHY
*And* HAND LETTERING

·TYPEFACE·

FREEHAND CAPITALS

UPPER CASE ⟷ WEIGHT: REGULAR ⟷ PUBLISHED: C. 1900

38

*Vault Editions Ltd*

PRACTICE
MAKES
PERFECT

INDUSTRY STD

VAULTEDITIONS.COM

·DESIGNER·
E. L. BROWN

# CALLIGRAPHY
## And HAND LETTERING

·TYPEFACE·
UNTITLED SCRIPT

UPPER CASE ←→ WEIGHT: REGULAR ←→ PUBLISHED: C. 1900

39

*Vault Editions Ltd*

CURATION AND RESTORATION SERVICES

PRACTICE
MAKES
PERFECT
TRD MRK

INDUSTRY STD

VAULTEDITIONS.COM

·DESIGNER·
E. L. BROWN

# CALLIGRAPHY
*And* HAND LETTERING

·TYPEFACE·
BUSINESS LETTERS

UPPER | LOWER | NUMERALS ⟷ WEIGHT: REGULAR ⟷ PUBLISHED: C. 1900

40

*Vault Editions Ltd*

PRACTICE
MAKES
PERFECT
T·R·D    M·R·K

INDUSTRY STD

VAULTEDITIONS.COM

CALLIGRAPHY
*And* HAND LETTERING

41

*Vault Editions Ltd*

PRACTICE
MAKES
PERFECT

INDUSTRY STD

VAULTEDITIONS.COM

·DESIGNER·
W. F. PARSONS

CALLIGRAPHY
And HAND LETTERING

·TYPEFACE·
ITALIAN CAPITALS

UPPER CASE   WEIGHT: REGULAR   PUBLISHED: 1890

42

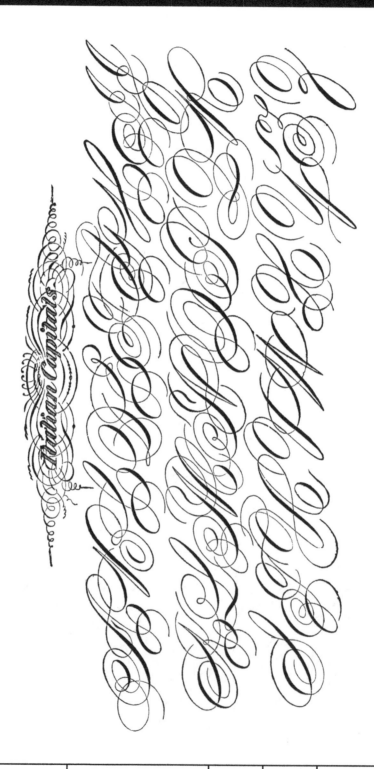

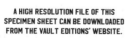
Vault Editions Ltd

PRACTICE
MAKES
PERFECT

INDUSTRY STD

VAULTEDITIONS.COM

·PUBLISHER·
LAIRD & LEE

CALLIGRAPHY
And HAND LETTERING

·TYPEFACE·
UNTITLED SCRIPT

UPPER CASE   ⟵ ⟶   WEIGHT: REGULAR   ⟵ ⟶   PUBLISHED: 1859

43

A B C D E F

G H I J K L

M N O P Q R

S T U V W X

a b c d Y Z e f g h

i j k l m n o p q r s t u v w

x y z 1 2 3 4 5 6 7 8 9 0

Vault Editions Ltd

PRACTICE MAKES PERFECT
T R D   M R K

INDUSTRY STD

VAULTEDITIONS.COM

·PUBLISHER·
LAIRD & LEE

CALLIGRAPHY
And HAND LETTERING

·TYPEFACE·
STANDARD CAPITALS

UPPER CASE ⟷ WEIGHT: REGULAR ⟷ PUBLISHED: 1859

44

Vault Editions Ltd

PRACTICE
T R D   MAKES   M R K
PERFECT

INDUSTRY STD

VAULTEDITIONS.COM

·PUBLISHER·
LAIRD & LEE

CALLIGRAPHY
And HAND LETTERING

·TYPEFACE·
UNTITLED SCRIPT

UPPER & LOWER CASE · WEIGHT: REGULAR · PUBLISHED: 1859

45

Vault Editions Ltd

CURATION AND RESTORATION SERVICES

PRACTICE
T R D · MAKES · M R K
PERFECT

INDUSTRY STD

VAULTEDITIONS.COM

·DESIGNER·
J. FRENCH

# CALLIGRAPHY
### And HAND LETTERING

·TYPEFACE·
ITALIC SCRIPT &
FLOURISHES

LOWER CASE ←→ WEIGHT: REGULAR ←→ PUBLISHED: 1854

46

PRINT.

ITALIC

*abcdefghijklm*

*nopqrstuvwxyz*

*Vault Editions Ltd*

CURATION AND RESTORATION SERVICES

T R D PRACTICE MAKES PERFECT M R K

INDUSTRY STD

·DESIGNER·
G. A. GASKELL

CALLIGRAPHY
And HAND LETTERING

·TYPEFACE·
ITALIAN ALPHABET

UPPER & LOWER CASE ←→ WEIGHT: REGULAR ←→ PUBLISHED: 1805

47

Vault Editions Ltd

PRACTICE MAKES PERFECT

INDUSTRY STD
VAULTEDITIONS.COM

.DESIGNER.

D. W. EDWARD

.TYPEFACE.

RUSTIC SCRIPT &
FLOURISH OF A SWAN

UPPER CASE ⟷ WEIGHT: REGULAR ⟷ PUBLISHED: 1859

48

47

A HIGH RESOLUTION FILE OF THIS
SPECIMEN SHEET CAN BE DOWNLOADED
FROM THE VAULT EDITIONS' WEBSITE.

*Vault Editions Ltd*

PRACTICE
MAKES
PERFECT

INDUSTRY STD

VAULTEDITIONS.COM

CALLIGRAPHY
And HAND LETTERING

49

Vault Editions Ltd

PRACTICE
MAKES
PERFECT

INDUSTRY STD

VAULTEDITIONS.COM

·DESIGNER·

D. W. EDWARD

CALLIGRAPHY
And HAND LETTERING

·TYPEFACE·

PRACTICAL LETTERING &
FLOURISH OF A SWAN

UPPER CASE ← → WEIGHT: REGULAR ← → PUBLISHED: 1859

50

Vault Editions Ltd

PRACTICE
T R D        M R K
MAKES
PERFECT

INDUSTRY STD

VAULTEDITIONS.COM

.DESIGNER.

D. W. EDWARD

CALLIGRAPHY
And HAND LETTERING

.TYPEFACE.

ORNAMENTED CAPITALS

51

Vault Editions Ltd

PRACTICE
TRD MAKES MRK
PERFECT

INDUSTRY STD

VAULTEDITIONS.COM

·DESIGNER·
KNOWLES AND MAXIM

CALLIGRAPHY
And HAND LETTERING

·TYPEFACE·
RUSTIC SCRIPT

UPPER CASE ⟷ WEIGHT: REGULAR ⟷ PUBLISHED: 1881

52

Vault Editions Ltd

CURATION AND RESTORATION SERVICES

TRD PRACTICE MAKES PERFECT MRK

INDUSTRY STD

VAULTEDITIONS.COM

.DESIGNER.
E. L. BROWN

CALLIGRAPHY
And HAND LETTERING

.TYPEFACE.
ORNAMENTED CAPITALS

UPPER CASE ←→ WEIGHT: REGULAR ←→ PUBLISHED: C. 1900

53

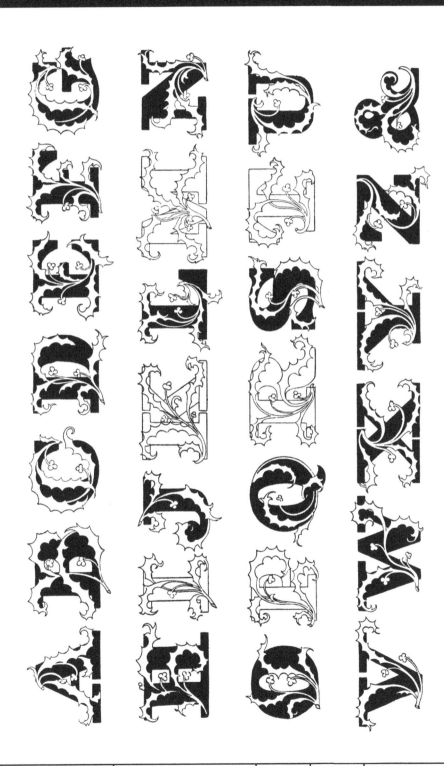

Vault Editions Ltd

PRACTICE MAKES PERFECT

INDUSTRY STD

VAULTEDITIONS.COM

## PUBLISHER.
### LAIRD & LEE

## CALLIGRAPHY
*And* HAND LETTERING

## .TYPEFACE.
### ROUND HAND FOR
### HEADINGS & DISPLAY

UPPER & LOWER CASE ← → WEIGHT: REGULAR ← → PUBLISHED: 1859

54

*ABCDEFGHIJK
LMNOPQRSTU
VWXYZ abcdefgh
ijklmnopqrstuvwxyz&:*

**53**

A HIGH RESOLUTION FILE OF THIS SPECIMEN SHEET CAN BE DOWNLOADED FROM THE VAULT EDITIONS' WEBSITE.

*Vault Editions Ltd*

PRACTICE MAKES PERFECT

INDUSTRY STD

VAULTEDITIONS.COM

·PUBLISHER·
LAIRD & LEE

CALLIGRAPHY
And HAND LETTERING

·TYPEFACE·
MODIFIED ROUND HAND

55

ABCDEFGHIJK
LMNOPQRSTUVVU
XYZ abcdefghijklm:
nopqrstuvwxyz.

Vault Editions Ltd

PRACTICE
MAKES
PERFECT
TRD MRK

INDUSTRY STD

VAULTEDITIONS.COM

· PUBLISHER ·
LAIRD & LEE

CALLIGRAPHY
And HAND LETTERING

· TYPEFACE ·
MEDIAEVAL

UPPER & LOWER CASE ← → WEIGHT: REGULAR ← → PUBLISHED: 1859

56

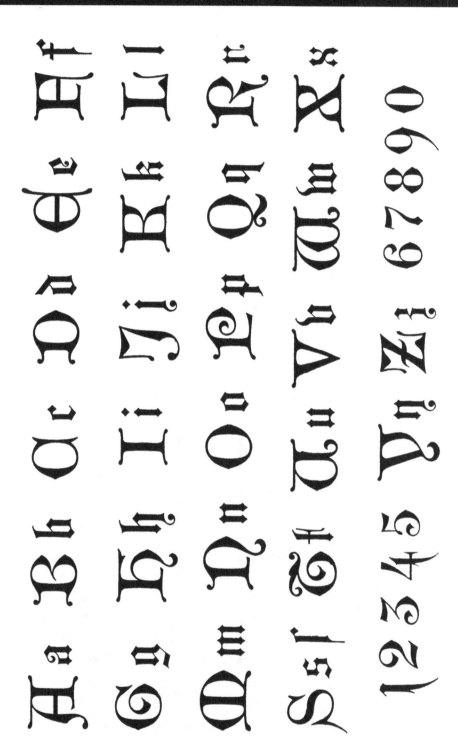

*Vault Editions Ltd*

PRACTICE MAKES PERFECT

INDUSTRY STD

VAULTEDITIONS.COM

.PUBLISHER.
LAIRD & LEE

CALLIGRAPHY
And HAND LETTERING

.TYPEFACE.
FANCY CAPITALS

UPPER | LOWER | NUMERALS  ←  →  WEIGHT: REGULAR  ←  →  PUBLISHED: 1859

57

A B C D E F G
H I K L M N O
P Q R S T U V
1 W X Y Z 2

a b c d e f g h i j k l
m n o p q r s t u v
3 4 5 6 w x y z 7 8 9 0

Vault Editions Ltd

CURATION AND RESTORATION SERVICES

PRACTICE
MAKES
PERFECT

INDUSTRY STD

VAULTEDITIONS.COM

·DESIGNER·
E. L. BROWN

CALLIGRAPHY
And HAND LETTERING

·TYPEFACE·
BROAD PEN BLOCK

UPPER & LOWER CASE ⟷ WEIGHT: REGULAR ⟷ PUBLISHED: C. 1900

58

abcdefghijklmno
pqrstuvwxyz
ABCDEFGHIJKLM
NOPQRSTUVWXYZ

57

Vault Editions Ltd

PRACTICE
MAKES
PERFECT
TRD
MRK

INDUSTRY STD

VAULTEDITIONS.COM

.DESIGNER.
E. L. BROWN

CALLIGRAPHY
And HAND LETTERING

.TYPEFACE.
STRAIGHT LINE LETTER

UPPER & LOWER CASE ←→ WEIGHT: REGULAR ←→ PUBLISHED: C. 1900

59

STRAIGHT LINE LETTER

ABCDEFGHIJKLMNOPQRSTUVWXYZ

abcdefghijklmnopqrstuvwxyz

Vault Editions Ltd

PRACTICE
MAKES
PERFECT

INDUSTRY STD

VAULTEDITIONS.COM

·DESIGNER·
E. L. BROWN

CALLIGRAPHY
And HAND LETTERING

·FEATURED·
EXERCISES FOR
FLOURISHING

FLOURISHING ← → DESIGNED: USA ← → PUBLISHED: C. 1900

60

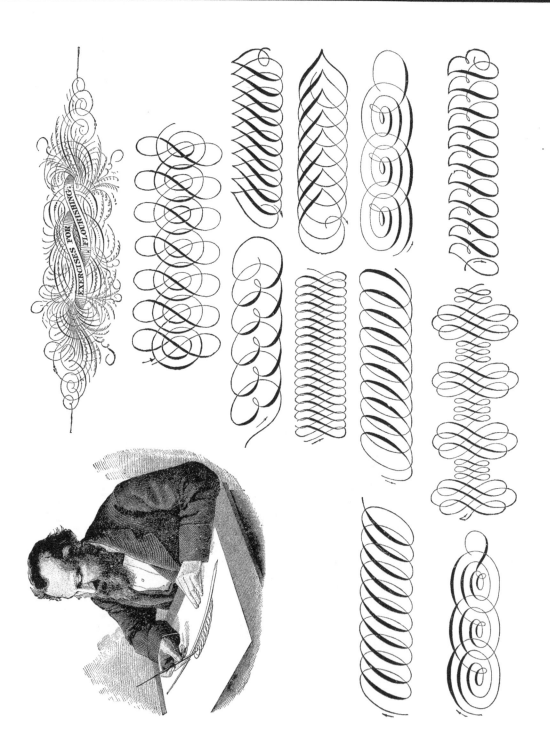

Vault Editions Ltd

PRACTICE
T R D MAKES M R K
PERFECT

INDUSTRY STD

VAULTEDITIONS.COM

.DESIGNER.

E. L. BROWN

CALLIGRAPHY
And HAND LETTERING

.FEATURED.

EXERCISES FOR
FLOURISHING

FLOURISHING ←——→ DESIGNED: USA ←——→ PUBLISHED: C. 1900

61

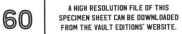

Vault Editions Ltd

CURATION AND RESTORATION SERVICES

PRACTICE
TRD MAKES MRK
PERFECT

INDUSTRY STD

VAULTEDITIONS.COM

.DESIGNER.
W. F. PARSONS

# CALLIGRAPHY
## And HAND LETTERING

.FEATURED.
EXERCISES FOR
FLOURISHING

FLOURISHING     ⟵ ⟶     DESIGNED: USA     ⟵ ⟶     PUBLISHED: 1890

62

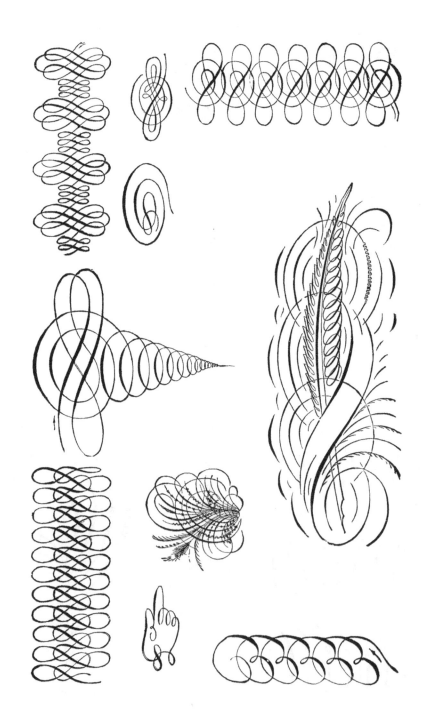

.DESIGNER.
W. F. PARSONS

.FEATURED.
EXERCISES FOR
FLOURISHING

FLOURISHING ← → DESIGNED: USA ← → PUBLISHED: C. 1900

63

Vault Editions Ltd

CURATION AND RESTORATION SERVICES

PRACTICE
T R D  MAKES  M R K
PERFECT

INDUSTRY STD

VAULTEDITIONS.COM

·DESIGNER·
G. A. GASKELL

CALLIGRAPHY
And HAND LETTERING

·FEATURED·
EXERCISES FOR
FLOURISHING

FLOURISHING      DESIGNED: USA      PUBLISHED: 1883

64

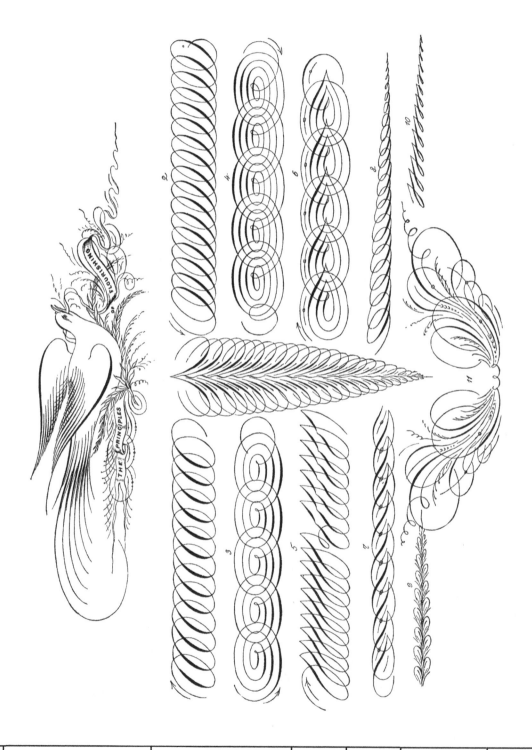

Vault Editions Ltd

PRACTICE
MAKES
PERFECT
TRD      MRK

INDUSTRY STD

VAULTEDITIONS.COM

·DESIGNER·
G. A. GASKELL

CALLIGRAPHY
And HAND LETTERING

·FEATURED·
FLOURISH STUDY OF AN
EAGLE & QUILL

FLOURISHING　　←→　　DESIGNED: USA　　←→　　PUBLISHED: 1863

65

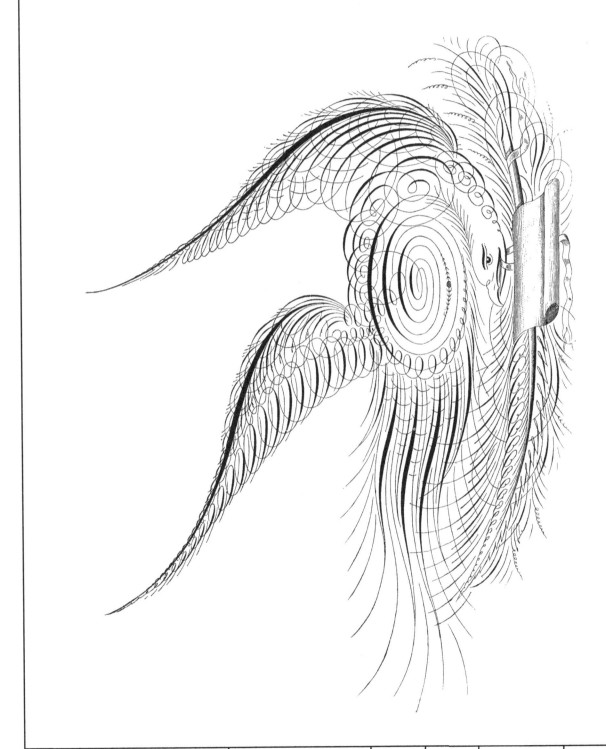

Vault Editions Ltd

PRACTICE
MAKES
PERFECT

INDUSTRY STD

VAULTEDITIONS.COM

.DESIGNER.
E. L. BROWN

CALLIGRAPHY
And HAND LETTERING

.FEATURED.
FLOURISH STUDIES
OF BIRDS

FLOURISHING ← → DESIGNED: USA ← → PUBLISHED: C. 1900

66

67

68

Vault Editions Ltd

PRACTICE
TRD MAKES MRK
PERFECT

INDUSTRY STD

VAULTEDITIONS.COM

.DESIGNER.
C. P. ZANER

CALLIGRAPHY
And HAND LETTERING

.FEATURED.
FLOURISH STUDIES
OF BIRDS

FLOURISHING · DESIGNED: USA · PUBLISHED: 1897

69

70

Vault Editions Ltd

PRACTICE
MAKES
PERFECT

INDUSTRY STD

VAULTEDITIONS.COM

.DESIGNER.
E. L. BROWN

CALLIGRAPHY
And HAND LETTERING

.FEATURED.
FLOURISH STUDIES
OF BIRDS

FLOURISHING ← → DESIGNED: USA ← → PUBLISHED: C. 1900

71

Vault Editions Ltd

PRACTICE
MAKES
PERFECT

INDUSTRY STD

VAULTEDITIONS.COM

·DESIGNER·
E. L. BROWN

# CALLIGRAPHY
*And* HAND LETTERING

·FEATURED·
FLOURISH STUDIES

FLOURISHING ← → DESIGNED: USA ← → PUBLISHED: 1897

72

*Vault Editions Ltd*

PRACTICE
MAKES
PERFECT

INDUSTRY STD

VAULTEDITIONS.COM

·DESIGNER·
C.P. ZANER

CALLIGRAPHY
And HAND LETTERING

·FEATURED·
FLOURISH STUDY
OF A RABBIT

FLOURISHING ←→ DESIGNED: USA ←→ PUBLISHED: C. 1900

73

Vault Editions Ltd

PRACTICE
T R D  MAKES  M R K
PERFECT

INDUSTRY STD

VAULTEDITIONS.COM

·DESIGNER·
C.P. ZANER

CALLIGRAPHY
And HAND LETTERING

·FEATURED·
FLOURISH STUDY
OF A DRAGON

FLOURISHING   DESIGNED: USA   PUBLISHED: 1897

74

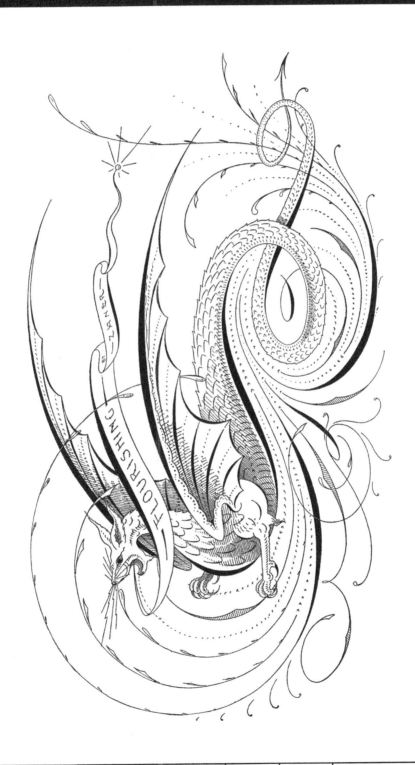

70

A HIGH RESOLUTION FILE OF THIS
SPECIMEN SHEET CAN BE DOWNLOADED
FROM THE VAULT EDITIONS' WEBSITE.

Vault Editions Ltd

PRACTICE
MAKES
PERFECT

INDUSTRY STD

VAULTEDITIONS.COM

·DESIGNER·
C.P. ZANER

# CALLIGRAPHY
## And HAND LETTERING

·FEATURED·
FLOURISH STUDY
OF A BIRD & WREATH

FLOURISHING      DESIGNED: USA      PUBLISHED: C. 1900

75

TO ALL        GOOD WILL

71

A HIGH RESOLUTION FILE OF THIS
SPECIMEN SHEET CAN BE DOWNLOADED
FROM THE VAULT EDITIONS' WEBSITE.

*Vault Editions Ltd*

PRACTICE
MAKES
PERFECT

INDUSTRY STD

VAULTEDITIONS.COM

·DESIGNER·
C.P. ZANER

·FEATURED·
FLOURISH STUDIES
OF VARIOUS BIRDS

FLOURISHING ← → DESIGNED: USA ← → PUBLISHED: 1897

76

77

Vault Editions Ltd

PRACTICE
MAKES
PERFECT

INDUSTRY STD

VAULTEDITIONS.COM

·DESIGNER·
C.P. ZANER

CALLIGRAPHY
And HAND LETTERING

·FEATURED·
FLOURISH STUDIES OF
A QUILL

FLOURISHING  DESIGNED: USA  PUBLISHED: C. 1900

78

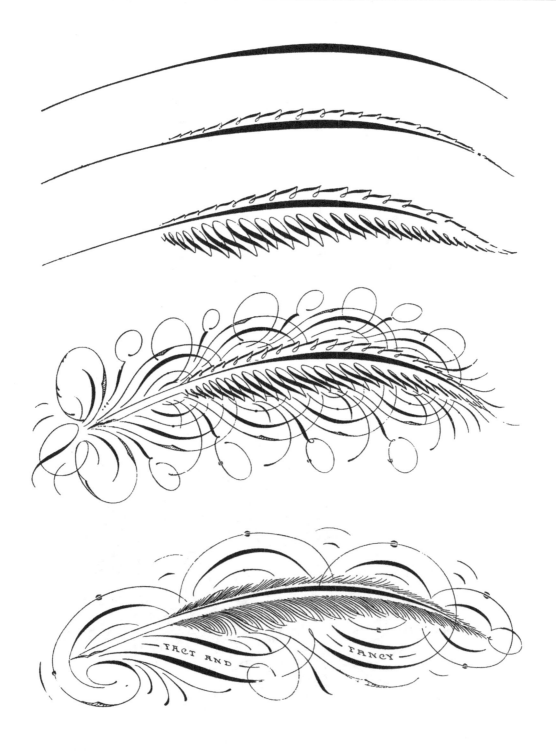

Vault Editions Ltd

PRACTICE
T R D  MAKES  M R K
PERFECT

INDUSTRY STD

VAULTEDITIONS.COM

·DESIGNER·
E. L. BROWN

CALLIGRAPHY
And HAND LETTERING

·FEATURED·
FLOURISH STUDY OF A
HORSESHOE

FLOURISHING  ←——→  DESIGNED: USA  ←——→  PUBLISHED: C. 1900

79

Vault Editions Ltd

PRACTICE MAKES PERFECT
INDUSTRY STD
VAULTEDITIONS.COM

· DESIGNER ·
E. L. BROWN

CALLIGRAPHY
*And* HAND LETTERING

· FEATURED ·
FLOURISH STUDY OF
A CORNUCOPIA

FLOURISHING · DESIGNED: USA · PUBLISHED: C. 1900

80

To catch Dame Fortune's golden smile
Assiduously wait upon her
And gather gear by every wile
That is justified by honor,
Not to hide in a hedge, nor for train attendant,
But for that glorious privilege
Of being INDEPENDENT

— ROBERT BURNS —

*Cornucopia*

*Vault Editions Ltd*

PRACTICE
MAKES
PERFECT
TRD MRK

INDUSTRY STD

VAULTEDITIONS.COM

·DESIGNER·
E. L. BROWN

CALLIGRAPHY
And HAND LETTERING

·FEATURED·
FLOURISH STUDIES OF
STAGS

FLOURISHING ←→ DESIGNED: USA ←→ PUBLISHED: C. 1900

81

82

Vault Editions Ltd

PRACTICE
TRD MAKES MRK
PERFECT

INDUSTRY STD

VAULTEDITIONS.COM

·DESIGNER·
E. L. BROWN

CALLIGRAPHY
And HAND LETTERING

·FEATURED·
FLOURISH STUDIES OF
BIRDS

FLOURISHING ←——→ DESIGNED: USA ←——→ PUBLISHED: C. 1900

83

FOR THE

BLACKBOARD

77

A HIGH RESOLUTION FILE OF THIS
SPECIMEN SHEET CAN BE DOWNLOADED
FROM THE VAULT EDITIONS' WEBSITE.

Vault Editions Ltd

PRACTICE
TRD MAKES MRK
PERFECT

INDUSTRY STD

VAULTEDITIONS.COM

.DESIGNER.
E. L. BROWN

CALLIGRAPHY
And HAND LETTERING

.FEATURED.
FLOURISH STUDIES OF
BIRDS

FLOURISHING ←→ DESIGNED: USA ←→ PUBLISHED: C. 1900

84

85

Vault Editions Ltd

PRACTICE
T R D   MAKES   M R K
PERFECT

INDUSTRY STD

VAULTEDITIONS.COM

·DESIGNER·
E. L. BROWN

CALLIGRAPHY
And HAND LETTERING

·FEATURED·
FLOURISH STUDY OF
A BANNER & BIRDS

86

Vault Editions Ltd

PRACTICE
MAKES
PERFECT

INDUSTRY STD

VAULTEDITIONS.COM

.DESIGNER.

E. L. BROWN

CALLIGRAPHY
And HAND LETTERING

.FEATURED.

FLOURISH STUDY OF
A BANNER & BIRDS

FLOURISHING ←→ DESIGNED: USA ←→ PUBLISHED: C. 1900

87

Vault Editions Ltd

PRACTICE
T R D MAKES M R K
PERFECT

INDUSTRY STD

VAULTEDITIONS.COM

·DESIGNER·
E. L. BROWN

CALLIGRAPHY
And HAND LETTERING

·FEATURED·
FLOURISH STUDY OF
AN ORNAMENTAL FRAME

FLOURISHING          DESIGNED: USA          PUBLISHED: C. 1900

88

Vault Editions Ltd

PRACTICE
T R D  MAKES  M R K
PERFECT

INDUSTRY STD

VAULTEDITIONS.COM

.DESIGNER.

E. L. BROWN

# CALLIGRAPHY
## And HAND LETTERING

.FEATURED.

FLOURISH STUDIES OF
ORNAMENTAL FRAMES

FLOURISHING　←→　DESIGNED: USA　←→　PUBLISHED: C. 1900

89

90

*Vault Editions Ltd*

CURATION AND RESTORATION SERVICES

PRACTICE
T R D MAKES M R K
PERFECT

INDUSTRY STD

VAULTEDITIONS.COM

·DESIGNER·
**KNOWLES AND MAXIM**

**CALLIGRAPHY**
*And* **HAND LETTERING**

·FEATURED·
**INSTRUCTIONAL DIAGRAM
FOR FLOURISHING A BIRD**

FLOURISHING  ⟷  DESIGNED: USA  ⟷  PUBLISHED: 1881

91

*Vault Editions Ltd*

CURATION AND RESTORATION SERVICES

TRD PRACTICE MRK
MAKES
PERFECT

INDUSTRY STD

VAULTEDITIONS.COM

·DESIGNER·
**KNOWLES AND MAXIM**

CALLIGRAPHY
*And* HAND LETTERING

·FEATURED·
**PARTS OF BIRDS**

92

*Vault Editions Ltd*

CURATION AND RESTORATION SERVICES

PRACTICE
MAKES
PERFECT
TRD MRK

**INDUSTRY STD**

**VAULTEDITIONS.COM**

·DESIGNER·
**KNOWLES AND MAXIM**

**CALLIGRAPHY**
*And* **HAND LETTERING**

·FEATURED·
**FLOURISHING STUDY OF
VARIOUS BIRDS**

**FLOURISHING** ⟷ **DESIGNED: USA** ⟷ **PUBLISHED: 1881**

93

*Vault Editions Ltd*

**PRACTICE**
**MAKES**
**PERFECT**

**INDUSTRY STD**

**VAULTEDITIONS.COM**

·DESIGNER·
**KNOWLES AND MAXIM**

**CALLIGRAPHY**
*And* **HAND LETTERING**

·FEATURED·
**FLOURISHING STUDY OF
A SWAN**

**FLOURISHING** ← → **DESIGNED: USA** ← → **PUBLISHED: 1881**

*Vault Editions Ltd*

PRACTICE
MAKES
PERFECT

**INDUSTRY STD**

**VAULTEDITIONS.COM**

·DESIGNER·
**KNOWLES AND MAXIM**

**CALLIGRAPHY**
*And* **HAND LETTERING**

·FEATURED·
**FLOURISHING STUDY OF
A BIRD & SCROLL**

**FLOURISHING** ←→ **DESIGNED: USA** ←→ **PUBLISHED: 1881**

95

*Vault Editions Ltd*

CURATION AND RESTORATION SERVICES

PRACTICE
T R D
MAKES
M R K
PERFECT

INDUSTRY STD

VAULTEDITIONS.COM

·DESIGNER·
**HNOWLES AND MAXIM**

CALLIGRAPHY
*And* HAND LETTERING

·FEATURED·
**FLOURISHING STUDY OF
A BIRD & BANNER**

FLOURISHING ←→ DESIGNED: USA ←→ PUBLISHED: 1881

96

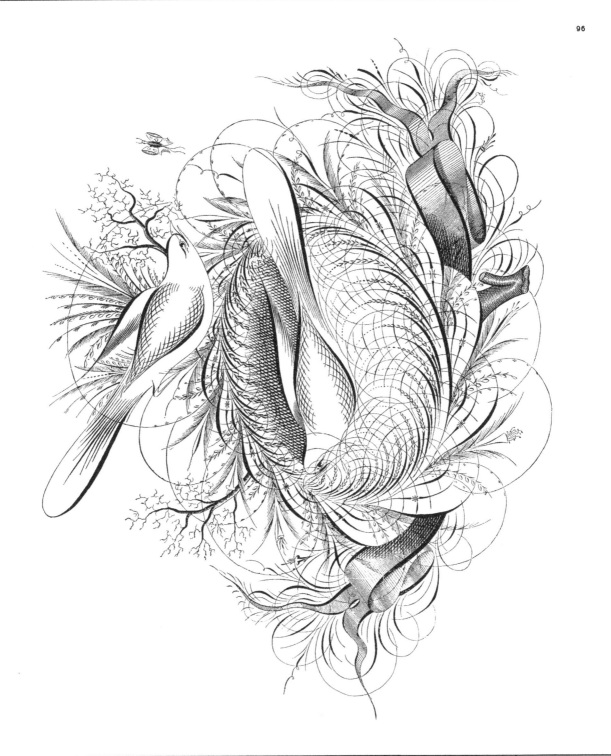

*Vault Editions Ltd*

PRACTICE
MAKES
PERFECT

INDUSTRY STD

VAULTEDITIONS.COM

·DESIGNER·
**KNOWLES AND MAXIM**

CALLIGRAPHY
*And* HAND LETTERING

·FEATURED·
**FLOURISHING STUDY OF HORSES**

FLOURISHING ←→ DESIGNED: USA ←→ PUBLISHED: 1881

97

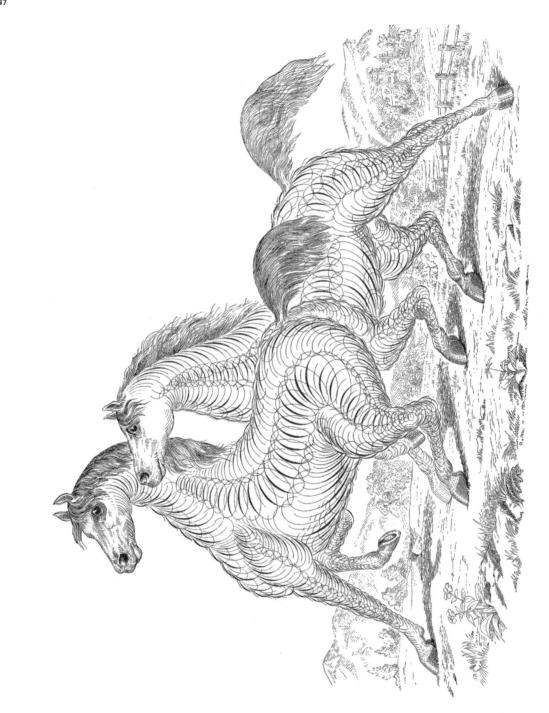

*Vault Editions Ltd*

CURATION AND RESTORATION SERVICES

PRACTICE MAKES PERFECT
T R D / M R K

INDUSTRY STD

VAULTEDITIONS.COM

·DESIGNER·
KNOWLES AND MAXIM

CALLIGRAPHY
And HAND LETTERING

·FEATURED·
FLOURISHING STUDY OF
DOGS ATTACHING A STAG

FLOURISHING ←——→ DESIGNED: USA ←——→ PUBLISHED: 1881

98

Vault Editions Ltd

CURATION AND RESTORATION SERVICES

PRACTICE
TRD MAKES MRK
PERFECT

INDUSTRY STD

VAULTEDITIONS.COM

·DESIGNER·
**KNOWLES AND MAXIM**

**CALLIGRAPHY**
*And* **HAND LETTERING**

·FEATURED·
**FLOURISHING STUDY OF
A HORSE**

FLOURISHING ←→ DESIGNED: USA ←→ PUBLISHED: 1881

99

REAL PENWORK

*Vault Editions Ltd*

CURATION AND RESTORATION SERVICE

T R D **PRACTICE**
**MAKES** M R K
**PERFECT**

INDUSTRY STD

VAULTEDITIONS.COM

·DESIGNER·
KNOWLES AND MAXIM

CALLIGRAPHY
And HAND LETTERING

·FEATURED·
FLOURISHING STUDY OF
A LION

FLOURISHING    DESIGNED: USA    PUBLISHED: 1881

100

REAL·PEN·WORK

Vault Editions Ltd

CURATION AND RESTORATION SERVICES

PRACTICE
TRD MAKES MRK
PERFECT

INDUSTRY STD

VAULTEDITIONS.COM

·DESIGNER·
**KNOWLES AND MAXIM**

**CALLIGRAPHY**
*And* **HAND LETTERING**

·FEATURED·
**FLOURISHING STUDY OF
A STAG**

FLOURISHING ⟷ DESIGNED: USA ⟷ PUBLISHED: 1881

101

*Vault Editions Ltd*

PRACTICE
MAKES
PERFECT

INDUSTRY STD

VAULTEDITIONS.COM

.DESIGNER.
HNOWLES AND MAXIM

.FEATURED.
FLOURISHING STUDY OF
AN EAGLE & SNAHE

FLOURISHING   ←→   DESIGNED: USA   ←→   PUBLISHED: 1881

102

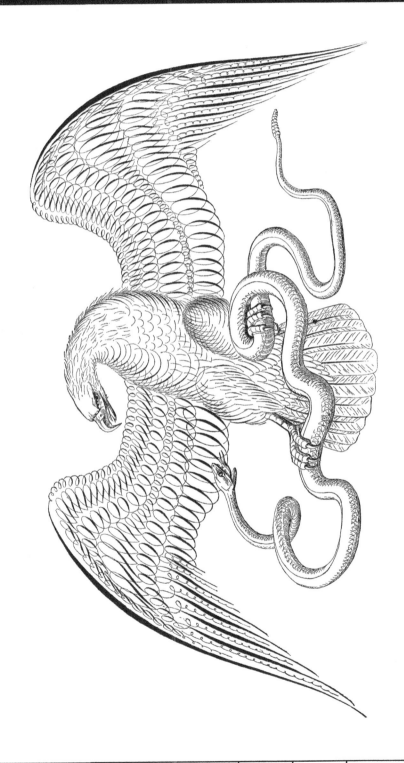

Vault Editions Ltd

PRACTICE
MAKES
PERFECT

INDUSTRY STD

VAULTEDITIONS.COM

· DESIGNER ·
**KNOWLES AND MAXIM**

**CALLIGRAPHY**
*And* **HAND LETTERING**

· FEATURED ·
**FLOURISHING STUDY OF
A FISH**

103

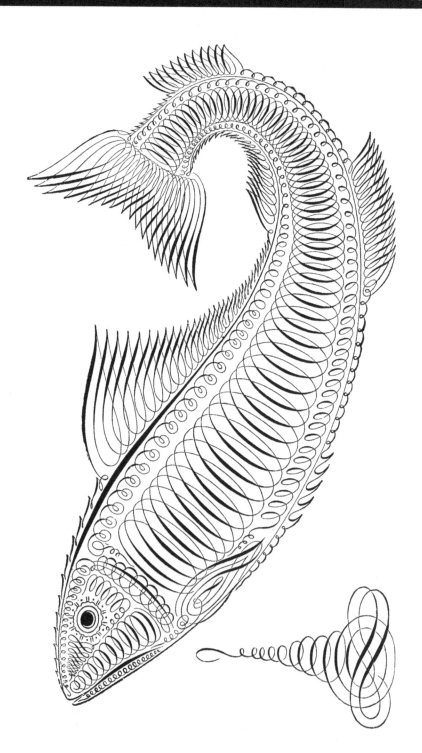

*Vault Editions Ltd*

**PRACTICE
MAKES
PERFECT**

**INDUSTRY STD**

**VAULTEDITIONS.COM**

·DESIGNER·
G. A. GASKELL

CALLIGRAPHY
And HAND LETTERING

·FEATURED·
FLOURISHING STUDY OF
A DRAGON

FLOURISHING  DESIGNED: USA  PUBLISHED: 1883

104

Vault Editions Ltd

PRACTICE
T R D  MAKES  M R K
PERFECT

INDUSTRY STD

VAULTEDITIONS.COM

·DESIGNER·
**KNOWLES AND MAXIM**

**CALLIGRAPHY**
*And* **HAND LETTERING**

·FEATURED·
**FLOURISHING STUDY OF
A BIRD**

**FLOURISHING** ← → **DESIGNED: USA** ← → **PUBLISHED: 1881**

105

**97**

A HIGH RESOLUTION FILE OF THIS
SPECIMEN SHEET CAN BE DOWNLOADED
FROM THE VAULT EDITIONS' WEBSITE.

*Vault Editions Ltd*

**PRACTICE
MAKES
PERFECT**

**INDUSTRY STD**

VAULTEDITIONS.COM

·DESIGNER·
**HNOWLES AND MAXIM**

**CALLIGRAPHY**
*And* **HAND LETTERING**

·FEATURED·
**FIGURATIVE FLOURISHING
STUDIES**

106

*Vault Editions Ltd*

PRACTICE
MAKES
PERFECT

INDUSTRY STD

VAULTEDITIONS.COM

·DESIGNER·
W. F. PARSONS

CALLIGRAPHY
And HAND LETTERING

·FEATURED·
FLOURISHING STUDY OF
BIRDS & BANNERS

FLOURISHING  ⟷  DESIGNED: USA  ⟷  PUBLISHED: 1881

107

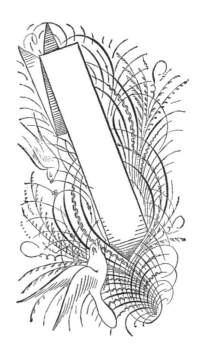

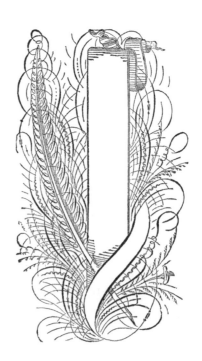

Vault Editions Ltd

CURATION AND RESTORATION SERVICES

PRACTICE
T R D  MAKES  M R K
PERFECT

INDUSTRY STD

VAULTEDITIONS.COM

·DESIGNER·
W. F. PARSONS

CALLIGRAPHY
And HAND LETTERING

·FEATURED·
FLOURISHING STUDY OF
BIRDS & BANNERS

FLOURISHING  ←→  DESIGNED: USA  ←→  PUBLISHED: 1881

108

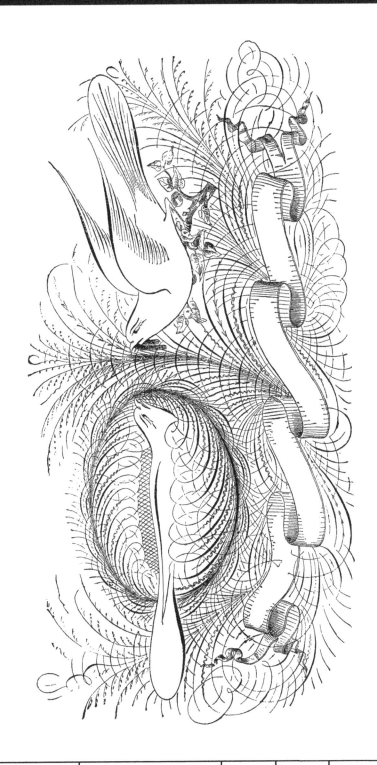

Vault Editions Ltd

CURATION AND RESTORATION SERVICES

T R D PRACTICE MAKES PERFECT M R K

INDUSTRY STD

VAULTEDITIONS.COM

·DESIGNER·
## W. F. PARSONS

CALLIGRAPHY
And HAND LETTERING

·FEATURED·
## FLOURISHING STUDY OF
## BIRDS & BANNERS

**FLOURISHING** ←——→ **DESIGNED: USA** ←——→ **PUBLISHED: 1881**

109

110

*Vault Editions Ltd*

PRACTICE
MAKES
PERFECT

INDUSTRY STD

VAULTEDITIONS.COM

·DESIGNER·
W. F. PARSONS

CALLIGRAPHY
And HAND LETTERING

·FEATURED·
FLOURISHING STUDY OF
BIRDS & BANNERS

FLOURISHING  DESIGNED: USA  PUBLISHED: 1881

111

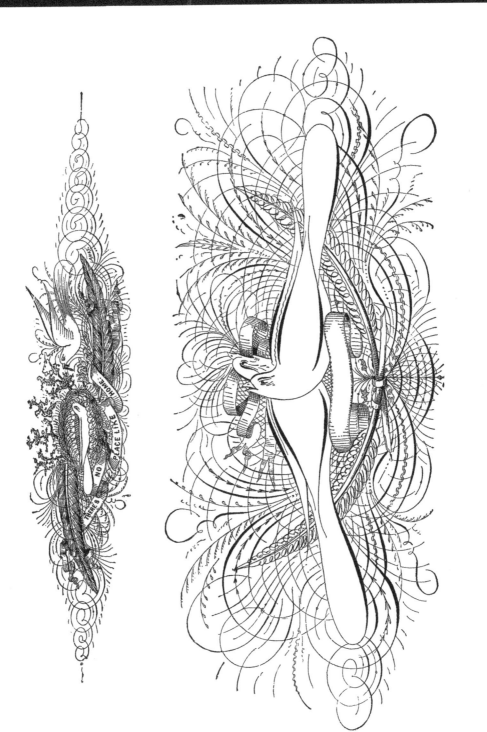

Vault Editions Ltd

PRACTICE
MAKES
PERFECT

INDUSTRY STD

VAULTEDITIONS.COM

·DESIGNER·
J. WISSLER

CALLIGRAPHY
And HAND LETTERING

·FEATURED·
FLOURISHING STUDIES

112

CHANGE.

PREM.

Vault Editions Ltd

PRACTICE
T R D   MAKES   M R K
PERFECT

INDUSTRY STD

VAULTEDITIONS.COM

·DESIGNER·
J. WISSLER

·FEATURED·
FLOURISHED TITLE PAGE OF
A FRENCH WORK

FLOURISHING ← → DESIGNED: USA ← → PUBLISHED: 1837

113

Vault Editions Ltd

PRACTICE
MAKES
PERFECT

INDUSTRY STD

VAULTEDITIONS.COM

·DESIGNER.
M. RISTER

# CALLIGRAPHY
### *And* HAND LETTERING

·FEATURED.
ORNAMENTAL ELEMENTS

ORNAMENTATION ←→ DESIGNED: USA ←→ PUBLISHED: 1883

114

*Vault Editions Ltd*

AND RESTORATION
CURATION SERVICES

PRACTICE
MAKES
PERFECT
TRD MRK

INDUSTRY STD

VAULTEDITIONS.COM

·DESIGNER·

A. CAULO

# CALLIGRAPHY
## *And* HAND LETTERING

·FEATURED·

ORNAMENTAL DESIGNS

ORNAMENTATION ←→ DESIGNED: USA ←→ PUBLISHED: 1883

115

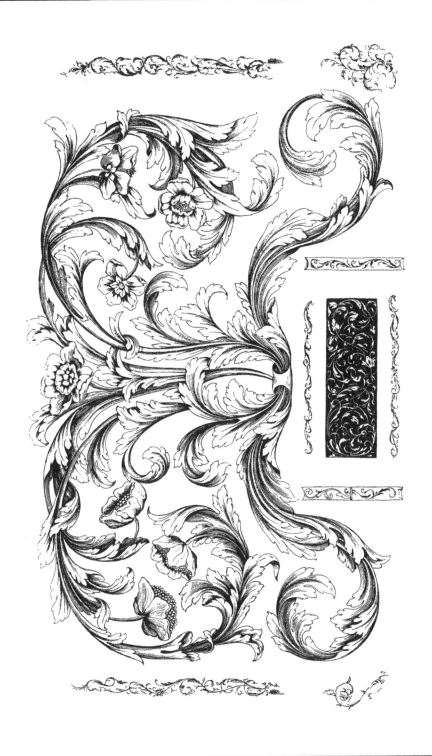

*Vault Editions Ltd*

CURATION AND RESTORATION SERVICES

PRACTICE
MAKES
PERFECT
TRD · MRK

INDUSTRY STD

VAULTEDITIONS.COM

·DESIGNER·
V. DHAUTEL

CALLIGRAPHY
And HAND LETTERING

·FEATURED·
CARTOUCHE DESIGNS

ORNAMENTATION ← → DESIGNED: USA ← → PUBLISHED: 1883

116

Vault Editions Ltd

PRACTICE MAKES PERFECT
TRD MRK

INDUSTRY STD

VAULTEDITIONS.COM

·DESIGNER·

V. DHAUTEL

CALLIGRAPHY
And HAND LETTERING

·FEATURED·

CARTOUCHE DESIGNS

ORNAMENTATION    DESIGNED: USA    PUBLISHED: 1883

117

Vault Editions Ltd

PRACTICE
T R D   MAKES   M R K
PERFECT

INDUSTRY STD

VAULTEDITIONS.COM

· DESIGNER ·
RIESTER

CALLIGRAPHY
And HAND LETTERING

· FEATURED ·
CARTOUCHE &
ORNAMENTAL ELEMENTS

ORNAMENTATION ← → DESIGNED: USA ← → PUBLISHED: C. 1800

118

109

A HIGH RESOLUTION FILE OF THIS
SPECIMEN SHEET CAN BE DOWNLOADED
FROM THE VAULT EDITIONS' WEBSITE.

Vault Editions Ltd

PRACTICE
TRD MAKES MRK
PERFECT

INDUSTRY STD

VAULTEDITIONS.COM

·DESIGNER·

REGINER

·FEATURED·

CARTOUCHE &
ORNAMENTAL CORNERS

ORNAMENTATION      ⟵⟶      DESIGNED: USA      ⟵⟶      PUBLISHED: C. 1800

119

*Vault Editions Ltd*

PRACTICE
MAKES
PERFECT

INDUSTRY STD

VAULTEDITIONS.COM

· DESIGNER ·
REGINER

CALLIGRAPHY
And HAND LETTERING

· FEATURED ·
ORNAMENTAL ELEMENTS

ORNAMENTATION ← → DESIGNED: USA ← → PUBLISHED: C. 1800

120

Vault Editions Ltd

PRACTICE
MAKES
PERFECT

TRD MRK

INDUSTRY STD

VAULTEDITIONS.COM

·DESIGNER·
M. RISTER

CALLIGRAPHY
And HAND LETTERING

·FEATURED·
ORNAMENTAL ELEMENTS

ORNAMENTATION ← → DESIGNED: USA ← → PUBLISHED: 1843

121

*Vault Editions Ltd*

PRACTICE
MAKES
PERFECT

INDUSTRY STD

VAULTEDITIONS.COM

·DESIGNER·
L. FEUCHERE

# CALLIGRAPHY
## And HAND LETTERING

·FEATURED·
FLORAL ORNAMENTAL
DESIGN

ORNAMENTATION  ←→  DESIGNED: USA  ←→  PUBLISHED: C. 1800

122

*Vault Editions Ltd*

PRACTICE
MAKES
PERFECT
TRD    MRK

INDUSTRY STD

VAULTEDITIONS.COM

·DESIGNER·

RIESTER

·FEATURED·

FLORAL ORNAMENTAL
DESIGNS

ORNAMENTATION ←——→ DESIGNED: USA ←——→ PUBLISHED: C. 1800

123

*Vault Editions Ltd*

PRACTICE
MAKES
PERFECT

INDUSTRY STD

VAULTEDITIONS.COM

·DESIGNER·
RIESTER

CALLIGRAPHY
And HAND LETTERING

·FEATURED·
ORNAMENTAL PANEL
DESIGN

ORNAMENTATION ⟵ ⟶ DESIGNED: USA ⟵ ⟶ PUBLISHED: C. 1800

124

Vault Editions Ltd

CURATION AND RESTORATION
SERVICES

PRACTICE
T R D MAKES M R K
PERFECT

INDUSTRY STD

VAULTEDITIONS.COM

·DESIGNER·
M. RISTER

CALLIGRAPHY
And HAND LETTERING

·FEATURED·
ORNAMENTAL DESIGNS

ORNAMENTATION ←→ DESIGNED: USA ←→ PUBLISHED: 1845

125

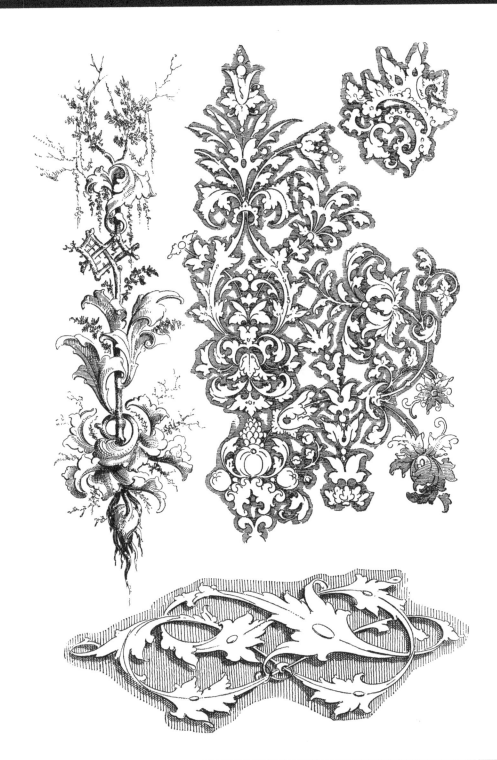

Vault Editions Ltd

PRACTICE
T R D MAKES M R K
PERFECT

INDUSTRY STD

VAULTEDITIONS.COM

.DESIGNER.
M. RISTER

CALLIGRAPHY
And HAND LETTERING

.FEATURED.
ORNAMENTAL PANEL &
ORNAMENTAL DESIGNS

ORNAMENTATION          DESIGNED: USA          PUBLISHED: C. 1800

126

Vault Editions Ltd

PRACTICE
T R D    MAKES    M R K
PERFECT

INDUSTRY STD

VAULTEDITIONS.COM

·DESIGNER·

L. FEUCHERE

# CALLIGRAPHY
## *And* HAND LETTERING

·FEATURED·

ORNAMENTAL DESIGNS

ORNAMENTATION ←→ DESIGNED: USA ←→ PUBLISHED: C. 1800

127

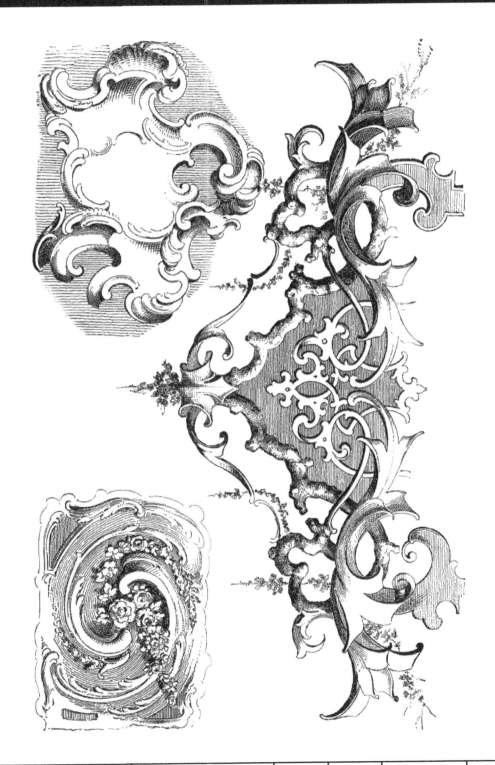

*Vault Editions Ltd*

PRACTICE
TRD MAKES MRK
PERFECT

INDUSTRY STD

VAULTEDITIONS.COM

**01**

**VOLUME**

**V A U L T   E D I T I O N S**

## VAULT EDITIONS

This publication is a new work created by Vault Editions Ltd

## DOWNLOAD YOUR FILES

Follow the instructions below to access your downloadable files

## LEARN MORE

At Vault Editions, our mission is to create the world's most comprehensive collection of image archives for the practical use of artists and designers. If you have enjoyed this book, you can discover more of our titles at vaulteditions.com

## REVIEW THIS BOOK

As a family-owned and operated independent publisher, reviews are essential to the success of our business. Please leave an honest review of this book wherever you purchased it.

## JOIN OUR COMMUNITY

Are you the creative and curious type? If so, you will love our community on Instagram. Every day, we share bizarre and beautiful artwork ranging from 17th and 18th-century natural history and scientific illustrations to mythical beasts, ornamental designs, anatomical drawings and more; join our community of 280K+ people today by searching @vault_editions on Instagram.

## STEP ONE

Enter the following web address on a desktop or laptop computer in your web browser.

vaulteditions.com/pages/cah

## STEP TWO

Enter the following password to access the download page:

**cahl27362838sxda**

## STEP THREE

Follow the prompts to access your high-resolution files.

## CONTACT

For technical support, please email: info@vaulteditions.com

Made in the USA
Las Vegas, NV
23 December 2024

15306411R00070